EXPRESSWAY TO READING

by

Beatrice G. Davis, M.S., P.D.

101 Creative Activities
to Put Readers
in the Fast Lane to Literacy

STECK-VAUGHN
BERRENT
PUBLICATIONS

Y0-DWN-448

Expressway to Reading

STECK-VAUGHN
BERRENT
PUBLICATIONS

ISBN# 0-7398-1894-5
Copyright ©1996 Steck-Vaughn Company.

All rights reserved. No part of this book may be reproduced or utilized in any form or by any means, electronic or mechanical, including photocopying, recording, or by any information storage and retrieval system, without permission in writing from the publisher. Inquiries should be addressed to: Copyright Permissions, Steck-Vaughn Company, P.O. Box 26015, Austin, TX 78755.

Published by Steck-Vaughn/Berrent Publications, a division of Steck-Vaughn Publishing Corporation.

1 2 3 4 5 6 7 8 9   00 99

Table of Contents

Introduction

We live in a print-dominated environment. As we move into the twenty-first century, literacy skills will be more important than ever before. It's doubtful that anyone will be able to succeed in life without having some ability to read. Schools provide children with the necessary skills for literacy learning, but children get the greatest benefit from what they learn in school when they practice at home. This means that parents should be actively involved in helping their children become independent, lifelong readers.

Parents are their children's primary teachers. Once children start school, parents must be involved in their children's education. The activities provided in this book will help you become full and effective partners.

Some Guidelines

While involved in the learning activities in this book or any others, try to keep them pleasurable and free from tension for your child. Avoid making them a continuation of school.

Remember to. . .

- Offer praise, using words like "great," "good job," "terrific," and "you're doing so well." *Honest* praise is one of the best motivators for learning.
- Be patient. Learning to read is a difficult task for some children. Oftentimes many repetitions are needed before a particular skill is learned. Success may not always be achieved on the first, second, or even third attempt.

- Make sure your child feels successful. Concentrate on activities in which s/he can get approximately eighty percent of the attempts correct.
- Always try to end an activity on a successful note. The last attempt is the one most likely to be remembered.
- Share the joys of reading by talking about and reading books together.
- Reading ability is improved by reading, not by doing pages in a workbook. So encourage your child to "Keep on reading!"

 Throughout the book, this "auto" icon will appear to the right of any activity that you and your child can do in the car.

Chapter 1

Developing Language by Reading Together

Learning to read is a natural process of speaking, listening, and writing. Literacy learning is helped by many different experiences with language. The more language experiences children have, the better chance they have of becoming successful readers.

One of the easiest ways to prepare your children for reading success in school is to read with them at home. Reading to your children will help expand their concept of the world and the language we use to communicate in and about it. Read with your children regularly. It is a positive way to perfect language skills.

1. Become Your Child's Literacy Learning Partner

Although your child may now be reading independently, s/he can still gain a great deal when you read to or with her/him. Choosing books based on your child's age and interest rather than reading ability exposes her/him to a wider variety of information and experience.

2. Establish a DEAR Time at Home

DEAR stands for Drop Everything And Read. Plan to spend at least 15 uninterrupted minutes each day reading a book or story that you both enjoy. Decide on a special reading place where you and your child can be comfortable while reading together. Maintaining a regular reading pattern + limiting television time could = an interested reader.

Note: Be sure to talk about the book you are reading. Talking about and reacting to books and stories can clarify meaning and improve comprehension.

3. Book and Story Questions

Questions such as "Why do you think the boy's mother. . . ?" "What would you do if. . . ?" or "What do you think will happen next?" help children to focus on the meaning of a story. Encourage them to develop questions, too.

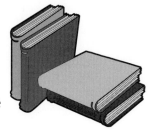

4. Tell It Again

Ask your child to retell a story in her/his own words. This is a valuable activity for developing comprehension skills. It requires paying attention to the details and the sequence of events in a story.

5. Invest in Reference Books

Your child should own a dictionary, preferably one at her/his grade level. If you can afford it, purchase a good set of encyclopedia. The Encyclopedia Buying Guide, which you can find in most libraries, is a helpful reference. Ask a teacher or the school librarian for help in making your choice.

6. Tape Record a Book

If you find that you're unable to read with your child on a regular basis, try making a tape of a book or story. If your child is a beginning reader, you could use signals, such as a whistle or bell, to indicate when a page should be turned.

7. Support Independent Word Attack

Try not to interrupt or make corrections while your child is reading to you. By not interrupting, you help develop awareness that the rest of the sentence will provide additional information. Encourage getting meaning from the rest of the sentence or story by saying "go on." If s/he insists that you help with a word or phrase, do so without comment. Your goal is to help your child become an independent reader.

8. Try to Make a Story Come Alive

You can make a story more exciting by using hand or finger puppets to retell or act out the plot.

9. Read Stories in Unison

Some stories are fun to read in unison. Choose a story or poem with which your child is familiar, and read it aloud together.

10. Preview a Book Together

Before you start to read a book, talk about the title, the pictures, and anything else that might be a clue to what the story is about.

11. Special Occasion Reading

 Start a family tradition of reading a favorite book for each holiday, birthday, or other special event that you celebrate together.

12. Read a Chapter at a Time

If you're reading a book that has several chapters, decide in advance how many you will read at each sitting. Before reading each chapter, be sure to talk about the events that happened in the previous chapters. This is helpful for understanding the sequence of events (the order in which a story happens) and learning how to summarize information.

Variations:

    I. Alternate silent and oral reading of a chapter.

    II. Act out various parts of the story before starting to read the next chapter.

    III. Before finishing the end of a chapter, ask your child to decide on some possible endings. Check to see how close s/he comes to the author's ending.

13. Read Special Story Parts

    A. Decide which parts of a story are most interesting. Read only these parts.

    B. Read only descriptive parts.

    C. Read provocative conversational passages.

    D. Read humorous incidents.

14. Newspaper Reading

Read the newspaper together. Talk about an interesting article. Encourage your child to find some of the details you talked about. Talk about the "Five Ws" of newspaper articles. They tell *who, what, when, where,* and *why* something happened.

15. More Newspaper Reading

A. Read the advertisements before you go shopping.
B. Read the captions under pictures to find out what a story is about.
C. Read the comics to follow a sequence of events and to predict what will happen next.
D. Read special sections, such as sports or science, that are interesting to you and your child.

16. What's in the Newspaper?

Browse through your local newspaper with your child. How many different parts does the paper have? How do you know where to find an article in which you're interested?

17. Encourage Regular Library Use

Using the library can have a positive effect on children's school work. It puts them in touch with books, media, and people who can help them. As soon as your child is eligible, be sure that s/he gets a library card. Of course, you should have one, too. Plan regular visits together.

18. Enroll Your Child in a Book Club

Encourage your child to order books from one of the many paperback book clubs that are used by the schools.

19. Start Your Own Book Club

Allow your child to purchase a book a month to add to her/his personal library. Once children have mastered the basics of reading, they often like to read books that are part of a series. Books in the *Danny Dunn*, *Amelia Bedelia*, and *Little Bear* series are very popular. Ask your child's teacher to recommend other series that are age and interest suitable.

20. Subscribe to Children's Magazines

The many children's magazines available have a great variety of stories, poems, puzzles, and activities for all ages. Check with your librarian or your child's teacher to get the names of the periodicals that would be most appropriate.

21. Let's Pretend

Allow your child to be a favorite book character for a day. Talk about what kind of clothes s/he would wear, special things s/he would do, what s/he would say.

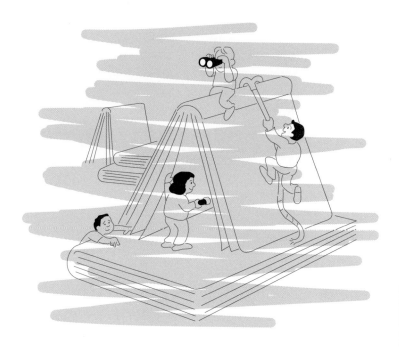

Chapter 2

Your Home as a Literacy Learning Center

Your home contains many wonderful, inexpensive educational materials. You just need to know what they are and how you can use them. This chapter lists some of the everyday items you can use.

22. Telephone Directory

Use your telephone directory to find last names of people that are the same as:
A. flowers,
B. colors,
C. fruits,
D. first names.

23. More Directory Activities

A. Use the telephone directory to find the many different kinds of doctors that are listed.
B. Select a page at random. What is the longest name on the page? The shortest name? The name that has the most vowels? The name that has the fewest vowels?
C. Find out whom you would call if:
a. your computer was broken.
b. you had a sick pet.
c. your bicycle needed to be repaired.
D. If your phone directory has a time-zone map, use it to find:
a. how many time zones there are in the country.
b. in which time zone you're located.

24. Use a Calendar to:

A. learn the spelling and abbreviations for days of the week and months of the year.
B. record the times of sunrise and sunset each day (found in most newspapers). You can then compute the amounts of daylight to see if days really do grow longer or shorter.

25. Greeting Cards

Use greeting cards to improve classification skills (the ability to group information under common headings). Cards can be grouped according to:
A. purpose (birthday, holiday, anniversary).
B. intended recipient (parent, child, grandparent).
C. rhyming or non-rhyming.
D. humorous or serious.

26. Other Greeting Card Activities

A. Hunt for the rhymes. Make a list of all the pairs of rhyming words that your child can find in greeting cards. What rhyming words can be added to the list?
B. Write original greeting cards using the words on the list.

27. Using Catalogs

A. Skim through mail-order catalogs to find descriptive words for various products.
B. Look for the same items in several catalogs. Compare prices, sizes, and colors of items described.
C. Talk about and make "Wish Lists" based on items in the catalogs.

28. How Do You Use It?

Directions on food packages, cleaning products, and the like are important sources of reading material. Read them to find out how to use a particular product. Read them to find out the correct order of steps that must be followed when using that product. After you and your child have read the directions together, try "testing" each other orally. "What has to be done first?" "Next?" "After that?" "Last?"

29. Family Alphabetical Order

(Do this activity only if you are sure that your child understands the meaning of alphabetical order.) Say the first names of several family members in random order. Ask your child to say the names back to you in alphabetical order.

Caution: Be sure to use names that start with different letters of the alphabet. Alphabetizing to the second or third letter is much more difficult. Don't expect your child to do this until s/he is very competent at first letter only alphabetical order.

Variations:

    I. Ask your child to arrange a group of toys according to the first letter of their names.

    II. Arrange fruits, vegetables, or any household items in alphabetical order.

    III. Start by saying a list of words such as apple, boy, car. Your child must say a word that would come next in order.

30. Collecting Things

Children are great collectors. Collecting such things as picture postcards, miniature cars, stamps, sports cards, dolls, and coins all require literacy skills, such as classification, reading for information, and comparing and contrasting.

31. What Does the Label Say?

Is something washable? Of what is it made? From what country does it come? All of these questions and more can be answered by reading labels and hang tags on clothing.

32. Using Television

A. Your television set can be a learning tool. After your child has watched a program, ask her/him to tell you five words that describe a character or situation.

B. Watch a commercial together. What was advertised?

C. Classify the kinds of programs your family likes to watch. Some classifications could be comedy, mystery, cartoons, or sports. Ask your child to look at a television schedule and find programs that fit each category.

D. Assign a different color pen or pencil to each member of the family. Have each person go through the television schedule circling the programs s/he likes to watch.

33. For What Are They Used?

Have your child sort and arrange cooking utensils, gardening tools, and any other tools used in your home, according to their use. This is good practice for using classification skills.

34. Look at the Birdie

If you own an inexpensive camera, your child can learn to use it. Pictures s/he takes can be given titles. Stories can be written or told about the pictures. Place them in a photo album with notes about the time and place they were taken. This is good preparation for record keeping.

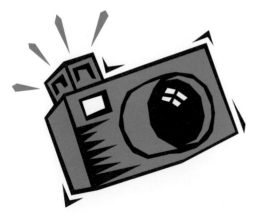

Chapter 3
Vocabulary Development

Vocabulary is considered the single most important factor in reading growth. If children are to become good readers, they need large and varied vocabularies. Reading ability improves as children add to their vocabulary words that they can recognize and understand.

35. Words That Tell About

Encourage your child to keep lists of "Words That Tell About" in a special notebook. For example: "Words That Tell About People," "Words That Tell About Time," "Words That Tell About Space," "Words That Tell About Travel." Add to the lists and create new ones as your child learns new words.

Variations:

   I. Make a list of season words: summer words, winter words, autumn words, spring words. These word lists will be useful in writing activities.
   II. List the words in alphabetical order.

36. Personal Word Banks or Files

A. Help your child to become a word collector. Words can be "deposited" in a small notebook. Each word can be entered on a separate alphabetical page. The definition and a sentence for the word can be written on the page also.

B. Buy 3x5 index cards. Your child can write each new word and its definition on the front of a card. One or two original sentences using the word can be written on the back of the card. Store the cards in an index card box or a shoebox. As new words are added, it will be easy to rearrange the cards in alphabetical order.

C. When a sufficient number of words are collected, they can be sorted into categories. Some categories might include: Feeling Words, Action Words, Happy Words, Sad Words.

37. Word Classification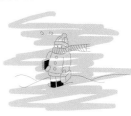

Say a series of words that can be classified as a group. Your child must think of the name of each group.

Examples:
crib, playpen, highchair, rattle = baby things
mittens, hat, scarf, down jacket = winter clothes

Variations:
   I. Include one word that doesn't belong with the others.
   II. Encourage your child to keep a notebook of words or pictures of things that go together.

38. Categories

Think of a category, such as flowers, foods, games. Take turns supplying words that fit the category.

39. Labels

Ask your child to make a label for each item on a shelf or in a cabinet.

40. Concentration

Materials: 3x5 index cards
Directions: Make two cards for each word that your child can read. Spread the cards face down on a table. The object of the game is to guess where the like cards are and to pick up matching pairs. Each player turns over two cards and reads the words aloud. If they match, the player keeps the cards and goes again. If they don't match, the cards are replaced and the next player takes a turn.

41. Word Battle

Materials: 40 or more 3x5 index cards

Directions: Divide the cards into two sets of twenty. Write a sight word and number (1 to 10) on each card in one set or pack. Write the same words and numbers on the cards in the second pack.

Give each player a pack, which must be kept face down on the table. At the word "go," each player turns over a card and says the word on it. The card with the larger number wins. The winner keeps both cards and places them on the bottom of her/his stack. The players keep turning over cards. If the cards they turn over have matching words or numbers, they have a word battle. Each player must then turn over and say the words on three cards. The numbers are totaled and the player with the highest number keeps all eight cards. If the totals are equal, a second battle is declared. Play continues until one player has all the cards.

42. Hunt for the Word

Decide on a topic for the day. Write several words about the topic on a sheet of paper. Your child must then search for and circle the words in newspapers and magazines.

Example:

The topic could be "Travel." Words such as *car, hotel, plane, trip, flight,* and *adventure* could be circled.

Variation: Restaurant Word Hunt

Tell your child to look for words that describe food s/he would order in a restaurant. Which food would be good to order for breakfast? For lunch? For dinner?

43. Words That Sound Like What They Say

Some words are made by imitating the sound associated with the object or action involved. This is called *onomatopoeia*. How many "sound words" can your child name?

Examples:
crunch, hiss, pop, buzz, jingle

44. Words in Hiding

Many long words contain letters that spell shorter words. It's fun to see how many words can be found in such words as "gingerbread" and "elephant."

> **Note:** Older children might decide to find only words that have three or more letters in them.

45. Which Word?

Select sentences from a book. Write them on a sheet of paper. Omit one word and draw a line in its place. Write two words under the sentence. Your child must choose the correct word and write it on the line.

Examples:
Sally planted pretty _____ in the garden.
(flowers, feathers)
Dogs like to _____ on bones.
(chase, chew)

46. Say It Another Way

Talk about common adjectives such as *big, little, pretty, funny, good*. Make a list of at least five other words that would say the same thing. This is a good pre-writing activity. Your child might want to keep a notebook of "Words That Can Be Said Another Way."

47. Use the Word

Decide on a word for the day or week. Keep a record of how many times you and your child use the word.

48. Homophone Hunt

Homophones are words that sound alike but are spelled differently and have different meanings. How many pairs of homophones can your child find in a magazine, story, newspaper, or book?

Variations:

I. Say a sentence using a word that has a homophone. Your child must say another sentence using the homophone. For example, you say: "I bought this jacket because it was on sale. Your child says: "Did you ever sail a boat?"

II. Make a homophone dictionary. You'll need blank sheets of 9x12 paper folded in half. Tell your child to write a homophone on each side of the page, then draw a picture and write a sentence to show the different meanings.

49. Picture the Word

Words such as *stormy, cloudy, curly, fat*, and *huge* are fun to illustrate. Your child might enjoy collecting and illustrating similar words in a scrapbook.

50. What Do I Spy?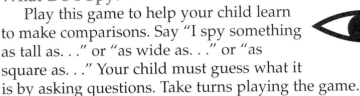

Play this game to help your child learn to make comparisons. Say "I spy something as tall as. . ." or "as wide as. . ." or "as square as. . ." Your child must guess what it is by asking questions. Take turns playing the game.

51. Riddle Me This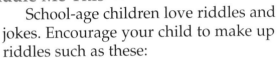

 School-age children love riddles and jokes. Encourage your child to make up riddles such as these:

What has legs but cannot walk? (a chair or table)
What has a tongue but cannot talk? (a shoe)

Variation:

Write and illustrate these riddles in a booklet. Write the question on one page with an illustration, then write the answer on the next page with another illustration.

52. Guess Who?

Take turns describing someone you both know without naming the person. Use as many descriptive words as you can. This is excellent preparation for writing.

Variation:

Describe a place to which you've both been.

53. Understanding Word Relationships

Make up sentences that will help your child see the connection between words. Ask her/him to tell you how the words are related.

Examples:
Hot is to cold as winter is to summer. (opposites)
Boy is to toy as bat is to cat. (rhymes)
Apple is to fruit as carrot is to vegetable. (classification)

Variation:
Leave out the last word of the sentence. Your child must say a word that will fit the relationship.

54. Tag It

Make tags, each with a description of a different item in a room. Don't include the names of the items in your descriptions. Ask your child to place the tags on the appropriate items.

55. Describe the Character

Ask your child to think of five words that describe a story character. Add the words to a word bank.

Variation:
Think of five words that are the opposite of the first five words.

56. Grow a Word

Start with several root words, such as *walk, talk, happy, laugh, take, mind.* Ask your child to add prefixes and suffixes (beginnings and endings) to the words (e.g. *walked, unhappy, laughing, mistake*).

57. Compound Words

Materials: index cards
Directions: Print a compound word (word formed by joining two words together) on each card (e.g. *schoolyard, airplane, baseball*). Cut the words apart. See how many new words your child can make by joining the cards together.

58. More Compound Words

Select a newspaper or magazine article, or a story in a book. How many compound words can your child find?

59. Take It

Materials: 3x5 index cards
Number of Players: two to four
Directions: Make four cards for each sight word or word in your child's word bank. Deal out six cards to each player. Place four cards face up on the table. Each player in turn checks to see if s/he has a card that matches one on the table. If so, s/he must show that card and say the word then keep both cards face up in a pile. If s/he does not have a matching card, s/he must place a card on the table. The next player checks the table and the piles in front of each player. If s/he has a match to any card showing, s/he may take the matching card after saying the word. The matching cards are then placed face up in front of the player.

60. Odd One

Materials: 3x5 index cards
Number of Players: two or more
Directions: Make four cards for each sight word or word in your child's word bank. Pick another word and make only one card for that word. Deal all the cards to each player. Each one in turn pulls a card from the hand of the player on the right. Whenever a player accumulates four matching cards, s/he must say the word, then place all four of the matching cards on the table. The game ends when only the "odd" card is left.

61. Go Fish

Materials: 3x5 index cards
Number of Players: two or more
Directions: Make four cards for each sight word or word in your child's bank. Deal five cards to each player. Place the remaining cards in a pile face down on the table. Each player asks the player on the right for a specific card by saying, "Do you have (word)?" The player who has been asked must give up all the cards that s/he has with that word on it. If s/he does not have the word, s/he says "Go fish." The asking player then "fishes" a card from the pile on the table. Each time four matching cards are accumulated, they are placed on the table. Play ends when all the cards are in sets.

Chapter 4

Phonics and Word Attack Activities

Phonics (the sounds that letters make), configuration clues (the shape of words), and structural analysis (prefixes and suffixes added to root words), are tools used to aid reading competence. The letters of our alphabet don't have a one-to-one letter/sound relationship. The 26 letters make more than 40 sounds, so children have to learn about letter/sound relationships.

62. Let's Eat

Choose an initial consonant for the day. Ask your child to find pictures of foods or food words that start with the letter you've chosen.

Example:
P: pizza, pasta, pears, pie

63. Tic-Tac-Toe

Materials: paper and pencils

Directions: Each player draws a tic-tac-toe grid on paper. The first player says a letter of the alphabet. Both players then write the letter in one of the grid squares. The second player says a letter, and both players enter the new letter in another square. Continue to alternate saying letters until all nine squares on both grids are filled. The player who can form the most words from the letters written on her/his grid wins. Words can be read from left to right, top to bottom, and diagonally from left to right.

64. Build a Word

Write a vowel (a, e, i, o, u) on paper, slate, or any other surface. Players take turns adding one letter at a time, making a new word each time. Pick a new vowel when no more words can be formed.

Examples:
a-at-hat-heat-wheat, o-go-goo-good-goody,
i-in-fin-fine-finer

65. Add a Letter

Come up with a list of words whose meanings can be changed by adding a letter at the beginning or end.

Examples:

(c)oat	Add a letter to make something to wear.
(w)easel	Add a letter to make an animal.
plan(t)	Add a letter to make something that grows.
(b)room	Add a letter to make something used to clean.

66. Phonic Fish

Materials: small magnet, string, two-foot-long stick, metal paper clips, construction paper, bowl or carton

Directions: Cut out small fish from construction paper. Write a short word on each fish (*cut, hip, tag, log, pen*). Put a clip through the mouth of each fish, and place the fish in the bowl or carton. Tie the magnet on one end of the string and attach the other end of the string to the stick. The players "fish" using this pole.

Variation:

Place a numerical value on the back of each fish. Establish a point system to earn specific rewards.

67. Lost Children

Choose a word family ending (e.g. *-all, -ick, -end*). Tell your child that Mr. and Ms. -ick (or one of the other word family endings) are ready to go on a picnic but they can't find all of their children. Help Mr. and Ms. -ick by listing as many words as possible that end with *-ick*.

68. Animal Tails

Materials: lightweight tagboard or construction paper

Directions: Cut out several different animals or several copies of the same animal. The animals should not have tails. Cut tails of various shapes. On each animal write a root word (e.g. *walk, play, tall, bang*). On each tail write an ending (e.g. *-ing, - est, -ed, -er*). The player must then place a tail on an animal to make a new word.

69. Rhyme Time

Say a word that has an ending that rhymes with other words (e.g. *back, fun, sing, rant*). Each player in turn must say a word that rhymes with the first word. The player who cannot think of a word gets the letter "r." A new word is chosen and the same procedure is followed. Each time someone is unable to say a word, another letter of the word *rhyme* is added.

70. Alphabet Action

Your child learns the alphabet and the sounds each letter makes by doing an action for each letter.

Example:
A: achoo, B: bounce, C: cut, D: dance, E: eat, and so on.

71. My Neighbor's Cat

Take turns describing "My Neighbor's Cat" by adding one word at a time in alphabetical order.

Example:
"My neighbor's cat is an angry cat." "My neighbor's cat is an angry, beautiful cat." "My neighbor's cat is an angry, beautiful, cuddly cat."

72. Holiday Games

Halloween: Look for words that rhyme with or start with *cat, witch, broom, pumpkin.*

Thanksgiving: Look for words that have the "ur" sound (as in *turkey*) in them or words that start with "th."

Christmas: Which toys would you get if Santa brought only short-vowel toys? Long-vowel toys?

Easter: Feed the bunny with words that start with "B."

73. Nonsense Poems

Make up nonsense poems using either short- or long-vowel rhyming words.

Examples:
If a pig wore a wig
He could dance a jig.

I can bake a cake that looks like a flake
When it floats on a lake.

74. What Do I Like?

Come up with a list of things you like that have double letters in the word. Say "I like cookies, but I don't like cake." "I like jelly, but I don't like jam." "I like feeling happy, but I don't like feeling glad."

Have your child use the same pattern to say what s/he likes.

75. Climb the Ladder

Materials: a sheet of paper, an envelope, word cards and/or pictures cut from magazines and newspapers, a pair of dice

Directions: Place the pictures or words you've selected into the envelope. Draw one or more ladders containing 12 steps on the paper.

Starting with the bottom step, number the rungs from 1 to 12. At the top of each ladder, write an initial consonant letter. Your child must roll the dice to find out how many pictures or words to find. S/He then "climbs up the ladder" to the rung with the number of pictures or words found.

76. Initial Consonant Day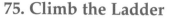

Decide on a letter for the day. How many things can your child identify that start with that letter?

Variations:

I. Limit the things found to one room in the house.
II. Find words or pictures starting with the chosen letter.
III. How many food words start with that letter?

77. Red Letter Day

How many things can your child find that start with the same letter as her/his name?

78. Alphabet Stories

Decide on a story letter. Every character, place, and name of object must start with that letter.

Examples:
Betty and Billy live in Boise. Betty has a big balloon. Billy has a big bat.

79. Fill in the Vowels

Write a sentence on a piece of paper eliminating all the vowels. See if your child can fill in vowels that will make sense in the sentence.

Example:
Sh_ p_t a d_me _n h_r p_ggy b_nk.

80. Make an Alphabet Scrapbook

Provide your child with a notebook in which s/he can paste pictures illustrating each letter of the alphabet.

81. "Magic E" Pencil

Write about 20 to 25 short-vowel words (usually made up of three letters, start and end with a consonant, and have a vowel in the middle) on a piece of paper. Tell your child that you are giving her/him a "Magic E" pencil that can change some of the words on the list. Explain that by adding only an "e" to the end of some words, you can create a new word. See how many words can be transformed.

Examples:
cap(e), mat(e), kit(e), rip(e), cut(e), hop(e)

82. Eagle Eye

Pick a letter. How many things starting with that letter can your child find when you're in the supermarket? In a toy store? A clothing store? Driving in the car?

83. Another Eagle Eye

Divide a piece of paper into two columns. Write "ea" at the top of one column and "gle" at the top of the other. Your child must use her/his "eagle eye" to find words in the newspaper that contain either of these phonic elements. They can be either cut out and pasted or written in the proper column.

Chapter 5

Comprehension Activities

Comprehension is the ability to understand what is read. This involves reading with a purpose or specific objective in mind, or using reading to fill in knowledge gaps. Your child should understand why s/he is reading and what it means.

84. Name That Picture

Look at a picture taken from a magazine or newspaper. Ask your child to list all the details s/he can find in the picture. When the list is complete, talk about the details that are important to the picture. Based on these details, ask your child to make up a title for the picture.

Variation:

When your child is able to read independently, have her/him make up titles for stories or paragraphs using the same technique of first listing the important details.

85. Stories in Order

Cut comic strips apart, then have your child put them together in the proper sequence.

Variation:

Ask your child to dictate a story for you to write. When it is finished, cut the story apart into single sentence strips. Your child can then make a book by pasting each sentence on a separate page and assembling them in order.

86. Surprise Box

Cut a hole in the lid of a shoebox. Place slips of paper with directions on them inside the box. Your child reaches in, takes out a slip of paper and follows the directions.

Example:
After you wash your hands, you may have a chocolate chip cookie and an orange.

87. What's in the Newspaper?

A. Use the paper to find out where a movie is showing.
B. Compare shopping prices by looking at the ads in the paper.
C. Cover the last part of a news article. See if your child can guess how the article might end.
D. Find out how many different datelines (the date and place the article was written) there are in the paper on a given day.

88. Solve the Problem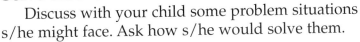

Discuss with your child some problem situations s/he might face. Ask how s/he would solve them.

Examples:
What would you do if you lost your key on your way home from school?
What would you do if you broke a neighbor's window?
What would you do if the power went off in the house?

89. Scrambled Sentences

Write a series of scrambled sentences on note paper. Ask your child to rewrite them.

Example:
her fell book shelf the off

90. Sentence Building

Pick a word that could be the first word of a sentence. Take turns adding a word to the sentence. The added word must begin with the last letter of the previous word.

Examples:
Seven naughty young girls sat together.
Books sometimes seem mysterious.

91. Charades

Write things to be acted out on pieces of paper.

Example:
"Make believe you're a firefighter."

92. Let's Cook

Give your child a simple recipe to follow. Let her/him assemble all the necessary ingredients and utensils. In addition to learning how to follow specific directions, your child will be able literally to taste success.

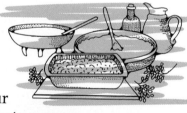

93. What's the Message?

Number each letter of the alphabet from 1 to 26. Write a message using numbers instead of letters.

Example:
3-15-13-5 6-15-18 4-9-14-14-5-18. (Come for dinner.)

Note: Be sure to leave a space between each group of numbers that stand for a word.

42

94. Where in the World?

Use a map or globe to locate the place where a specific story took place. Talk about:

A. what's special about that location,
B. what you know about that particular location,
C. where you could find more information about it.

95. Thinking and Reasoning

After you've read a story, ask your child to find sentences or words that tell:

A. how something or someone feels,
B. how something or someone looks,
C. what might happen next.

96. Clozing in on Meaning

(A cloze activity involves filling in a blank in a sentence with a word that makes sense. Many reading tests use this method to check comprehension.)

Cut out or copy a paragraph from an old book that your child no longer uses. Newspaper and magazine articles can be used, too. Leave the first and last sentence intact, then delete every fifth word. Your child must fill in the spaces with words that make sense in the story.

97. What's Next?

Start to tell a story. Stop, and ask your child to tell you what the next word should be.

98. Hunt for the "W's"

After you've read a story, ask your child to tell you:

A. *who* the story is about,
B. *what* the story is about,
C. *where* the story took place,
D. *when* the story took place.

99. Things That Go Together

Say or show your child a list of words that go together. Include one word that doesn't belong (e.g. *sled, snow, icicle, swimsuit*).

Variation:

> *Ask your child to make up similar lists. You must then guess the word that doesn't belong.*

100. Cause and Effect

Share nursery rhymes such as *Jack and Jill, Little Miss Muffet,* and *Hickory, Dickory, Dock* with your child, then talk about the causes or effects of specific events in the rhymes.

Examples:

Why did Jack break his crown? What happened when the spider sat down beside Miss Muffet? What made the mouse run down the clock?

101. Eating and Reading

Look at a cereal box. Of what is the cereal made? Is it sugar-coated or plain? In what city was it made? Can you send away for anything if you save the box top?

Some Phonic Definitions

The vowels are: *a, e, i, o, u,* and, sometimes, *y.*
The short vowel sounds are:
> *a* as in *apple*
> *e* as in *egg*
> *i* as in *inch*
> *o* as in *ox*
> *u* as in *umbrella*

The long vowels are:
> *a* as in *ate*
> *e* as in *even*
> *i* as in *ice*
> *o* as in *open*
> *u* as in *use*

The letters that are not vowels are called consonants.
Words that have a consonant-vowel-consonant pattern are always short (e.g. *can, hot, bug*).
Words that have two vowels between a beginning and ending consonant usually have the the long sound of the first vowel (e.g. *coat, bean, rain*)

Hard and soft *c* and *g*
1. The letters *c* and *g* usually have a soft sound when they come before the letters *e, i,* or *y.*
2. Soft *c* sounds like the letter *s* as in *cent.*
3. Soft *g* sounds like the letter *j* as in *age.*
4. When *c* and *g* come before other letters they usually have a hard sound as in *can* and *go.*

A PARENT'S

A is for Arms that hold a child with love.

B is for Books, which banish boredom.

C is for Caring for and Cherishing children.

D is for Doors, which books help open.

E is for Education, which happens at home as well as at school.

F is for the Freedom children must have to discover the world.

G is for Grandparents, who add wisdom to children's lives.

H is for Home, where children feel wanted and loved.

I is for Ignorance, which darkens the world.

J is for the Joy that comes from learning and living.

K is for Kids, who fly kites and kick balls.

L is for Love and Laughter and Life.

M is for Memories of shared moments.

ALPHABET

$\mathcal{N}$ is for Nurturing and caring.

O is for Openness, which children and parents must work at together.

$\mathcal{P}$ is for Parenting, which requires so much patience.

Q is for the Quiet times you spend with your child.

$\mathcal{R}$ is for the Reward that you get when you see your children reading independently.

S is for School, where you should visit often.

$\mathcal{T}$ is for Teachers, who are there for your child.

$\mathcal{U}$ is for Understanding, which you try so hard to show.

$\mathcal{V}$ is for the Vigor you need to get through each day.

$\mathcal{W}$ is for all the "Why's" one child can ask and for the Wisdom it takes to answer them well.

X is for the eXtra love and attention it takes to be a parent.

$\mathcal{Y}$ is for Youthful Years, which go by so fast.

Z is for the Zest for learning you instill in your child.